Every story starts its journey to immortality

the moment is written down

www.ingramcontent.com/pod-product-compliance
Lightning Source LLC
Chambersburg PA
CBHW060939120726
47910CB00002B/408

* 9 7 8 1 0 8 8 1 9 9 9 5 4 *